inside
handball

Paul Haber defeating Bill Yambrick for the USHA National Open Singles title, in Texas.

inside handball

paul haber

with

mort leve
executive secretary USHA and editor of ACE magazine

photographs by

arthur shay
contributing photographer SPORTS ILLUSTRATED

HENRY REGNERY COMPANY · CHICAGO

Published by Henry Regnery Company
    180 North Michigan Avenue, Chicago, Illinois 60601

Manufactured in the United States of America

Library of Congress Catalog Card Number: 72-126157

International Standard Book Number: 0-8092-8868-0 (cloth)
                                    0-8092-8867-2 (paper)

contents

tournaments won by paul haber

1966   Sea Fair Doubles (Paul Morlos, partner); Seattle, Washington

1966   Sun Fair Singles: Yakima, Washington

1966   Canadian National Doubles (Paul Morlos, partner): Vancouver, Canada

1966   Golden Gate Doubles (Paul Morlos, partner): San Francisco, California

1966   USHA National Singles: Salt Lake City, Utah

1967   World Open Doubles (Stan Garden, partner): Toronto, Canada

1967   Canadian National Singles: Montreal, Canada

1967   USHA National Singles: San Francisco, California

1967   Amarillo Invitational Singles: Amarillo, Texas

1967   Las Vegas Invitational Doubles (Dave Stewart, partner): Las Vegas, Nevada

1968   Tall Corn Invitational Singles: Des Moines, Iowa

1968   Oklahoma Invitational Singles: Oklahoma City, Oklahoma

1968   USHA National Contenders Doubles (Paul Morlos, partner): Seattle, Washington

1968   Milwaukee City Doubles (Barry Schwartz, partner): Milwaukee, Wisconsin

1969   Mardi Gras Invitational Singles: New Orleans, Louisiana

1969   USHA National Open Singles: Austin, Texas

1969   USHA National Invitational Singles: Birmingham, Alabama

1969   Bozo Invitational Doubles (Paul Morlos, partner): Odessa, Texas

1969   Rainbow Beach 3-Wall Doubles (Jack McDonald, partner): Chicago, Illinois

1970   USHA National Singles: Los Angeles, California

1970   National YMCA Singles: Chicago, Illinois

1970   USHA National 3-Wall Doubles (Andy Upatnieks, partner): Detroit, Michigan

1970   USHA National Invitational Doubles (Don Ardito, partner): Denver, Colorado

1971   USHA National Singles: Memphis, Tennessee

1971   USHA National Invitational Singles: Birmingham, Alabama

1971   USHA National 3-Wall Doubles (Andy Upatnieks, partner): Detroit, Michigan

1971   USHA National Round-Robin Singles: St. Paul, Minnesota

1972   National YMCA Singles: Norfolk, Virginia

foreword

It was in 1819 that William Hazlitt, the English critic, wrote: "It may be said that there are things of more importance than striking a ball against a wall—there are things indeed which make more noise and do so little good, such as making war and peace, making speeches and answering them, making verses and blotting them, making money and throwing it away. But the game of fives [handball] is what no one despises who has ever played it. . . . He has no other wish, no other thought, from the moment the game begins, but that of striking the ball, of placing it, of making it! It is the finest experience for the body, and the best relaxation for the mind. . . ."

It is now more than 40 years since I struck my first handball, and I am still having trouble "placing it" some three times a week. Still, I try, I aspire. And I count as some of the finest moments of my life those I've spent "striking a ball against a wall" in common with some of the five million or so other handball players in this country.

From among the thousands of happy handball duffers like myself, there occasionally arises a superior handball player who enters tournaments and achieves local renown on the courts. From these skilled few there then emerges another handball elite: the champions. Just as men compete in our somewhat better-known national mania, golf, these handball champions compete in national tournaments, are publicized in the national press and on television, and are a joy (and alas, often a heartache) to watch.

From these champions, one champion of champions has emerged. He is Paul Haber.

In the world of handball, Paul Haber is Arnold Palmer, Jack Nicklaus, Bobby Hull, Joe DiMaggio, Joe Namath, and a dash of Frank Sinatra. A *Sports Illustrated* writer has called him "the most colorful champion in sports since Namath—and with better knees."

It is a pleasure to introduce this instructional book, which is designed to bring the new player into the game via the Haber method and to help those of us already addicted to "striking a ball against a wall" for mere fun and exercise to improve our game skills.

The fraternity of handball is such that (aside from putting me in touch with William Hazlitt!) it has brought together Mort Leve, the United States Handball Association Secretary, who assisted with the text, Arthur Shay, the photographer who took the pictures, Paul Haber, and myself. While this book was being prepared Haber and Shay managed to beat Leve and me eight times straight in doubles. Shay discounts Haber's aid in the left court, preferring to attribute his victories to a careful reading of the manuscript.

Although you may never have Paul Haber as your left-court partner, his book should prove a more than adequate substitute.

Robert W. Kendler, Founder and President
United States Handball Association

acknowledgments

The author and photographer wish to thank these institutions for permission to take the photographs on their handball courts: Lake Forest College, Lake Forest, Illinois; YMCA, Northbrook, Illinois; YMCA, Birmingham, Alabama; University of Texas, Austin, Texas.

The photographs on the following pages were shot by Arthur Shay on assignment for *Sports Illustrated* and are reproduced here through its courtesy: Frontispiece, 29, 30, 31, 41, 44, 46, 48, 49, 68. Prints by Astra Labs., Chicago.

inside
handball

1

introduction to handball

The handball bug bites different people in different ways. It bit me at a very early age, but then I had the advantage of being born in New York City, where there are more than a thousand one-wall courts and where the deep sidewalks abutting tenement walls make perfect natural courts. (Dodging New York traffic, I've always suspected, provided an extra sharpening for my footwork.)

My father, Sam Haber, introduced me to four-wall handball at the famous Castle Hill Beach Club in the Bronx—a club most noted for its crowded swimming pool, but where handball was nonetheless king. My father was one of the city's best competitive players, and his friends at the club recall that when I brought my street-style play into a regulation court at Castle Hill Beach, I used to run around like a wild Indian until some of these experienced old-timers took me in hand. By the time we moved to Chicago—when I was ten years old—I was hooked on the game. I didn't so much take up handball as it took up me.

This brings us to the question: Why do *you* want to take up handball? The competition? The exercise? Why? Whatever your reason, or reasons, you've chosen an excellent sport. Handball is, first of all, a lot of fun, a sport that lets you play *your* game, without the regimentation of large-team

organization. It is also a superb physical conditioner, since it combines the exercise of running with the use of the coordinated skills common to all games played with a ball. In short, it is one of the most convenient ways to stay in shape there is. If you're a businessman, tired or otherwise, or a worker who once prided himself on staying in shape but has let himself slide, you'll find that handball is the kind of purposeful, driving, satisfying activity that makes an hour pass enjoyably while at the same time it tones and strengthens your muscles and builds your endurance. Calisthenics, wind sprints, and jogging are fine—but handball will do everything they can for you, and it's a lot more fun.

The fundamentals are really quite simple. Once learned, they serve as a foundation on which you can build as high as you like, from simple proficiency to competitive skills good enough to win tournaments.

Handball can be played on different kinds of courts—one-, three-, and four-wall —but because four-wall handball is the most popular variety, I am going to concentrate on it. Four-wall handball, then; and as a first piece of advice I'd like to suggest that you start thinking of four-wall handball as a *five*-wall game, because the ceiling should play an important part in your game strategy, as you will see.

1

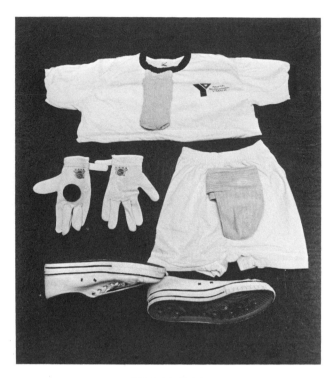

EQUIPMENT.

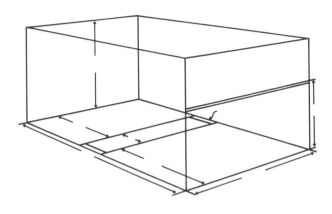

THE COURT.

Equipment

You don't need much: a pair of good-quality gym shoes (suit yourself as to whether they're high- or low-cut, but get a pair that won't slip on a wooden floor), sweat socks with a reinforced foot, an athletic supporter, shorts and T-shirt. If you wear glasses, they should be made out of plastic. Finally, you'll need deerskin or goatskin handball gloves and a standard handball. That's all. Your first few times on a court you won't even need an opponent.

The court

The regulation handball court is 20 feet wide and 40 feet long. Its front wall is 20 feet high and its back wall must be at least 12 feet high. The serving zone, 5 feet wide, extends across the width of the court, its rear (or "short") line lies 20 feet from the back wall and divides the court into equal front and back areas. The service line of the service zone is 15 feet from the front wall.

To reserve a court for practice or play, all that's necessary is to call the man who makes court assignments. Simple? Here's a further very worthwhile piece of advice: Stay on good terms with this man. Courts get booked up a long time ahead.

The game

The full rules of handball as set forth by the United States Handball Association can be found starting on page 54 of this book. Very briefly stated, they go like this: A game of handball begins with the server in the serving zone. He bounces the ball, then hits it. The server cannot step across the service line as he serves or he commits a fault. His serve must strike the front wall and then bounce back beyond the short line into the back court. If his serve strikes the ceiling, the rear wall, or three walls before it reaches the back court, he has committed a fault. Two faults while serving cost him the serve.

And a player can score in handball only when he is serving

The server's opponent—the receiver—must return the serve to the front wall, either directly or indirectly. That is, a return can hit the side walls before it reaches the front wall, or it can hit the ceiling, or even the back wall—but it cannot touch the floor before reaching the front wall. Nor can the receiver cross the short line until the ball has crossed the short line after a serve. Once a rally, a sequence of shots, has begun, either receiver or server can return a ball before it reaches the floor on its rebound from the front wall, and he *must* return it before it bounces against the floor twice.

The whole idea of the game of handball, then, is to keep returning that ball to the front wall. When the receiver fails to return the ball, the server scores a point. When the server himself fails to return the ball to the front wall, he loses the serve—and to repeat, a player scores in handball only when he is serving.

The first player to score 21 points in a game wins it.

Just a mention here of penalties (which are covered in full in the rules). The most controversial rule is the "avoidable" hinder. The theory is that each player is entitled to "a *fair* chance to *see* and to *return* the ball." When a player is denied this "fair chance" by his opponent, it is an avoidable hinder if the opponent could have moved sufficiently to give a clear shot.

Now, most handball games are played without a referee, the two (or four, sometimes three) players engaged in combat gentlemanly officiating their own game. But often, of course, the competitive flame is burning so brightly during a game that an argument will ensue over whether or not a hinder was actually avoidable. Well, they'll have to decide, but it leads to a lot of arguments.

On avoidable hinders that the server and his receiver can agree the server has made (or, in the instance of a refereed game, that the referee calls), the server loses the serve. If the offender is the receiver, the violation costs a point. Such avoidable hinders would be called when a player (1) doesn't move sufficiently to allow his opponent a shot, or (2) moves into a position that blocks his opponent's view of the ball, or (3) moves into the path of his opponent's return and is struck by the ball.

In serving, your opponent (or a referee) must decide whether your body "screens" your serve from his view. If judged a screen, a server must serve again—with no penalty.

There are other, less controversial hinders. If a ball *accidentally* strikes an opponent before reaching the floor, this is a hinder; so too is a player's *unintentional* interference with his opponent. In any case, no point is lost on such "dead-ball" hinders, as they are called; they are, as the kids say, "do-overs."

First steps for beginners

Before you even go near a handball court for the first time, have a complete physical. Let your doctor know that you are planning to take up handball, and he will advise you in accord with your physical condition on how to pace yourself for beginning to play the game. (It may be that he will prescribe a one- or two-week conditioning program for you.)

Once you step on a court, the very first thing to do—for beginner and experienced player alike—is to loosen up. I'd suggest that the first one or two times you step on a court you do so alone—and use the hour for solitary practice. But even when you're

THROWING BALL OVERHAND. Face the side wall. Get used to various straight and angle rebounds.

there to play, resist the temptation to begin a game as soon as you arrive. Instead, walk around the court a few times, jog in place awhile, flail your arms like a windmill (just as "Sugar Ray" Robinson used to before that first bell), do some kneebends. Bend from the waist and touch the floor a few times. Loosen up.

Clap your hands together a few times. Bounce the ball a few times and catch it. *Loosen up.* Right from the start, form good court habits, one of which should be: Start your motor slowly. Coax your muscles into action. Get your body working for you. Proficiency in handball depends on coordination and timing, not chiefly on power. (Power will come along on its own as your other skills develop.) When you shoot, don't try to murder the ball. Coax it into action without violent movements. The same applies to your body. Coax it into working for you. Loosen up.

Second steps

Do you remember when you were a kid and spent hours tossing a ball against a wall or against the front steps of your house— toss and catch, toss and catch? That was a fine introduction to handball, and it is also a fine way to warm up for a game after you're loose. Practice throwing the ball against the walls, bouncing it from wall to wall, from ceiling to floor, tracking it with your eyes and body as it rebounds, and then catching it. Start slowly, and keep your eye on the ball.

A handball usually comes off the wall at an angle exactly opposite to that at which it hits. Angle the ball from the front wall to the side walls a few times, each time trying to predict where the ball will hit the floor, and where you should be to play it. Skill in this comes largely as a result of practice,

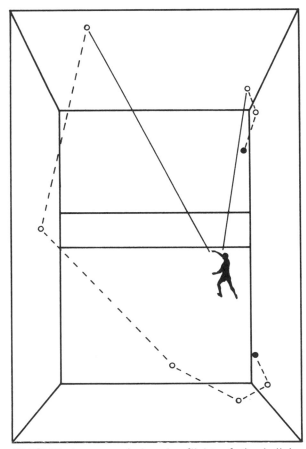

FLIGHT. Learn to judge the flight of the ball by throwing to the wall.

and after a time your eyes and hands and body will begin to function together automatically (just as they did when you learned to ride a bicycle); you won't have to think consciously of what you should do or of where the ball is going.

Alternate your warm-up throws so that you hit the front wall first, then a side wall first. Then hit it so that you use two or more walls—and don't forget the ceiling. Throw and throw and throw—toss and catch—using your natural, "stronger" arm. (I'll talk about your weaker, or "off," arm later.) In all of your throws, of course, try to make the ball hit that front wall before it strikes the floor, because ultimately that's what handball is all about.

Gradually you can increase the tempo of your warm-up throws, at the same time trying to increase your skill at predicting where the ball is going. As you speed up your throws, vary their height as well as their direction. Toss and catch, speeding up each toss just a little. Show your body that you mean business, but don't strain or over-extend yourself. Practice at least 25 of these accelerated throws. By the time you're finished, you may feel a little like an outfielder who's been put through wind sprints from one side of the field to the other—all day. But you also should have a pretty fair idea of where the ball is going, and what to do about it.

The off hand

Now run through the same warm-up with your weaker, or "off," hand (for most of us, our left hand). Discouraging, isn't it? Your throws resemble those of a not particularly agile, middle-aged woman.

Don't let it discourage you too much, though. In baseball that off hand is your catching hand; you can make it work for you in handball, too. Work to produce a mirror image of the motion and natural footwork that you use when you throw with your stronger arm. (Jim Jacobs, an all-time handball great, suggests practicing before a full-length mirror, copying with your off arm the natural action you see when using your stronger arm.)

Above all, don't worry about speed when you begin. Just work on your off-side motion and coordination. In remarkably short order—your body learns quickly—you will have developed an off hand that will keep you in all your games and may even win a few for you.

Never discount that off hand. Work on it. Play games against yourself, strong arm against weak; occasionally play games against an opponent in which each of you restricts himself to his weak arm. There are many points to be won, many saves to be made with that off hand.

Bob Kendler, President of the USHA and a longtime Masters player, refers to the natural hand as the sword, and the other one as the shield. I think he's right; basically, the off hand should be used as a shield—that is, for defense. (I've seen quite a few otherwise fine players try to use their off hand as an offensive weapon—as a sword—and lose points time and time again. But because the off hand is chiefly a defensive weapon is no reason to neglect it. It must be a smoothly moving shield.)

If you find yourself getting discouraged over the rate at which skill with your off hand is developing, or not developing, re-member George Quam. He lost an arm in an accident at the age of nine, took up handball at eighteen—against the advice of several physical education instructors—and ultimately his determination earned him the Minneapolis Athletic Club singles cham-pionship, a championship he won for 25 consecutive years. When Quam was in-stalled in handball's Hall of Fame he said, "I don't believe that having one hand has been a handicap. Every one of us was given at birth more natural ability, equipment, and talent than we will ever use in our lifetime. Your success is not going to be determined by what you have to work with—but by how you use what you have."

Think about that, and then practice the accelerated 25-throw warm up with your off hand; practice an alternate-shot (natural, then off-hand) drill; practice, practice, practice with your weak hand. After a time, though it will still be your weaker hand, it won't be weak.

Footwork

In handball, as in every other sport, proper footwork is the silent partner of

FOOTWORK. As you complete your swing, firmly plant your weight on your front (right) foot for an off-hand (left) shot. Your weight shifts from back to front foot. Vice versa for right-hand shots.

coordinated handwork. If you stand flat-footed and throw with the wrong foot leading, you will see from the results that this is so. (The results will resemble those that might be gotten by that not particularly agile, middle-aged woman.) During the throws you have been making with your stronger arm in your warm up, you should have been transferring your weight from your back (right) foot to your forward (left) foot at the moment of release. (I'm talking about right-handers; left-handers will have to interpret.)

Work for a smooth flow of movement from wind-up—however slight—through release and follow-through. At the instant you release the ball in your practice throws, your forward foot should be bearing most of your weight, just as a baseball player's does when he releases the ball. (This shift in weight is also very much like the classic transfer of force in golf, via the hips, from back to forward foot.) For most handball shots—or, at this stage, throws—the knees should be flexed slightly. For low throws—as you vary the height of your practice throws—the knees should be flexed a little more.

I'll spend more time on footwork in the next chapter, where the basic strokes are discussed, but for now let it be said—as Mike Dau, well-known Lake Forest College handball coach says—that the main function of footwork is to place your body so that a shot can be made by stepping into the ball as it passes the centerline of your body. Thus, in your warm-up throwing, practice releasing the ball at the moment your hand arcs past the centerline of your body.

Right-handed shot

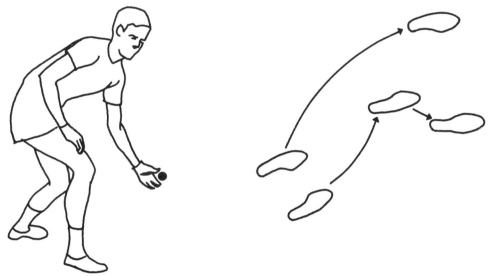

Left-handed shot

FOOTWORK. Correct footwork is essential. When making a shot with your right hand, your weight should be on your left foot at point of contact with the ball. Vice versa for left-handed shots.

2

the basic strokes

You are now ready to begin practicing the basic strokes used in hitting the ball. (Probably your hands are fairly soft. To keep them from bruising easily, soak them in hot water for about five minutes before starting practice.) There are three basic strokes used in handball—the overhand, the sidearm, and the underhand. The sidearm stroke is *the* stroke in handball, and a variation of it is usually used by most players in serving.

Overhand stroke

Ideally, the overhand stroke in handball should resemble the smooth, graceful overhand motion of a baseball pitcher, or the catcher's peg to second base, or the overhand tennis stroke. In *feel* there is an upward surge of the body that reaches a climax of power as hand meets ball. As you go to meet the ball, and your legs take you into hitting range, your arm (elbow bent, fingers together, flexing from full cup to slight cup just beyond the flat hitting surface of the upper palm) should arc to approximately six inches above your head and a similar distance from your ear. As your feet move forward with the overhand stroke, your weight should shift from back to front foot. At the moment of impact in the overhand stroke—as in almost every

9

other handball shot—the body should be facing one of the side walls.

You should attempt to reach the ball *before* you hit it (often, of course, this is not possible), delivering the overhand stroke— and the sidearm and the underhand—from a stationary position whenever possible, your footwork with the overhand stroke invariably moving you forward. If you've learned to predict the angle of rebound, and if you are anticipating your opponent's

shots with fair success, you'll be in position to do this a good percentage of the time. As I mentioned in Chapter One, the ball should be hit just as it reaches an imaginary line that runs outward and up and down from the centerline of your body.

Some of my students have found it helpful to imagine a rope suspended from about six inches above their heads and dangling about six inches in front of their noses down to their ankles. I then ask them to imagine

OVERHAND STROKE. Line up ball about a foot over your head, slightly in front of your body, using your off hand for balance. At point of contact, your weight shifts to your front (left) foot. The ball is struck where your palm and cupped fingers meet, rolling off your fingers for the needed "feather touch." The ball is stroked upward to the ceiling. Control is the major factor. Follow through smoothly.

that this rope races invisibly around the court with them as they play, and tell them to stroke the ball only when they think their stroke would pass through the invisible rope. (This is the centerline concept again.)

Most of the time when I use the overhand stroke as a return, I loft the ball to the ceiling (handball, remember, is a *five*-wall game). To do this, it is necessary to bend back slightly at the waist in order to get greater arm extension, but such a return leaves your opponent with a high, bouncing shot to return, a difficult shot to play, as you will no doubt discover. I also often use this overhand ceiling shot when I'm feeling tired. Its high trajectories and bounces give me both a little extra breathing time and also time to plan my next shot.

To practice hitting overhand ceiling shots, move to one side of the court or the

IDEAL POSITION. Let the ball descend and stroke it low, at knee height, with your body bent. Use the sidearm swing. Keep your eyes on the ball. Shift your weight from your back (right) to your front (left) foot.

INCORRECT STANCE. In each case, the arm is too close to the body, thus constricting smooth swing.

other and try to hit the ceiling a few feet from where it joins the front wall. The most difficult kind of overhand ceiling stroke of all to return is the one that comes off the front wall and then hugs one of the side walls as it returns to the back court. Try to aim your shots so that they do this—hug the walls. Developing this knack will prove of great value to your game.

Sidearm stroke

The sidearm stroke is the most effective stroke in handball, the most used. It is most used because with it you return shots before they pass you and become difficult to retrieve from the back court (particularly wall-angled shots).

The ball is struck, as usual, as it crosses the midline of your body—along that dangling rope, if you will. At the beginning of the sidearm stroke, the body is facing one of the side walls. As the ball is struck, the body turns toward the front wall in a movement similar to a pitcher's follow-through in baseball. The handball player, like the pitcher, ends up poised on the balls of his feet, facing front, ready for his next move. In baseball that move might be off the mound to field a bunt; in handball, of

SIDEARM STROKE. Meet the ball at the proper point of contact as your weight moves from your back to your front foot. Keep your body low, your swing parallel to floor, meeting the ball away from your body, at knee height.

course, the player is waiting for his opponent's next shot and hoping to put it away irretrievably.

Footwork for the sidearm shot is as customary—weight back, then—at contact—weight thrown forward. Gradually, after you've made hundreds of these shots, you will find yourself working more and more of your body's natural power into them.

Underhand stroke

The underhand stroke—*the* natural shot in handball—is used for digging a low ball off the floor. By "natural" I mean it is the kind of shot that kids in New York City, Detroit, and elsewhere develop while playing makeshift games against one wall. If

UNDERHAND STROKE. "Dig" ball, getting low. Keep your hand low, with your fingers toward floor. Meet the ball close to the floor. Following through with straight underhand swing, knees flexed, as low as possible.

you had the good fortune to grow up on city streets playing one-wall, the stroke will seem natural to you. Otherwise, it will require some practice, since about the only other sport I can think of that uses it is softball, and there it is the specialty only of the pitcher.

The underhand stroke uses the customary footwork of the other strokes, weight moving forward from back to front foot, with the ball hit at centerline about six inches from the body. As you begin the stroke you shift your weight to your back foot and swing your arm back into position. As your arm comes forward, so does your weight. Your arm follows through across the front of your body as your weight comes down on your front foot.

Unless you can put it away out of your opponent's reach with this shot, I don't recommend using the underhand stroke for rallying—that is, for exchanging shots with your opponent. All too often with it, you will simply give him a return he can murder. What the underhand stroke is especially good for is, as I said, digging out low balls and returning them to the front wall.

Some Irish players are quite adept at a variation of the underhand stroke called the "Irish whip," a whiplike underhand stroke together with a strong, circular wrist motion. The Irish, who are accustomed to larger courts (30x60 feet) than we play on, seem to use this shot more than half the time when they come to our smaller courts, and some of them have developed it into a deadly accurate weapon. Be that as it may, I recommend that you use your underhand stroke principally as a retriever of otherwise unreturnable shots thrust at you by your opponent. It is the last measure shot to return the ball.

Your sidearm stroke should be your artillery and frontline power. Your overhand

"BOLO" OR UPPERCUT SWING WITH FIST. Face side wall. Meet the ball at the "cuticles" of your fingers, hand clenched. Follow through.

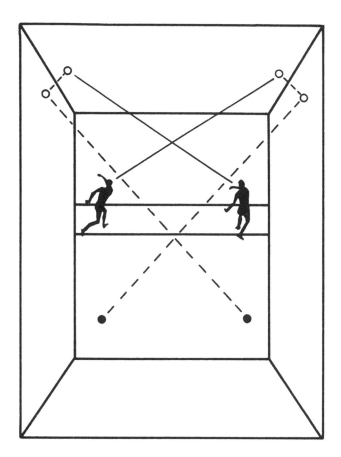

SERVICE. Two good serves are illustrated. The zigzag serve is especially effective.

should be used to weaken or delay your opponent, with the ceiling overhand used to give you time. Your underhand is used to get you out of trouble when you are under attack.

There are players—and you may be one of them—who violate these principles, but, by and large, winning handball consists of developing a full arsenal of the basic strokes and then using them properly as weapons of offense and defense. When you feel, in practice, that a stroke is working right for you, keep on practicing it. Try to duplicate it again and again. Try to master it. This is how you will gain control of your strokes.

Serving

Underhand, overhand, or sidearm, the server puts the ball into play from the server's box. Ideally, you serve the ball so that your opponent can't return it. Since you can score while you're serving—and only while you're serving—if you can serve the ball 21 times in a row, so that your opponent can't return it, you've got yourself the game. (First, of course, you've got to win the toss for serve. Unfortunately, I do not know of any method that guarantees success in this.)

But the serve, then, is of prime importance to your game, and it is, therefore, important to develop a good, offensive serve that is hard to handle, one that puts your opponent on the defensive right from the start. If you can develop such a serve, his returns will be much easier to handle than otherwise, and you may establish an edge that will give you an advantage throughout the game.

What is an effective serve? Any serve that your opponent has trouble handling.

You will come to the point where you will be able to evaluate your opponents as you play them so that you know their weaknesses. Then you serve to those weaknesses. But for a starter, serve to your opponent's weak hand consistently, until you are able to evaluate his game. And when you have him convinced that you are going to continue feeding to his off hand, give him a serve to his strong hand, especially if he has begun overplaying the off-hand portion of the court.

This raises an important point: In serving from spot to spot, change the speed of your delivery and the direction in which you hit. Look to one place, serve to another. Keep your opponent off balance, expecting one kind of serve, receiving another.

Practice all types of serves, using all three basic strokes. Try lobbing the ball high and making it hug a side wall on its rebound. (This is an excellent serving stroke, especially if your opponent has a very weak off hand.) Try a sidearm serve that shunts the ball low into one of the corners.

As you practice serves, concentrate on avoiding the serve that rebounds to the back court, bounces to the back wall, and comes off it in perfect position for your opponent's sidearm. Mix them up! Practice your aim. Pick out imaginary spots on the court and try to hit them with serves during your solo practice.

Try hitting an overhand "Z" serve. From the left-hand side of the serving box, hit the ball to the front wall, far to the right. The ball will carom from front to side wall, bounce in center court, and go back into the far-left, rear corner, where it will hit the left wall, then the rear wall, and finally (with luck or skill on your part) drop low, completing a "Z" pattern and presenting your opponent with a most difficult retrieve.

This serve must be hit with speed, however, and be placed accurately, or it gives the receiver a set-up—so practice, practice, practice!

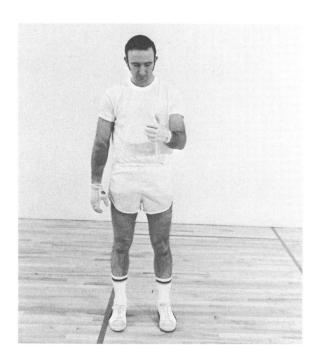

SIDEARM SERVE. Get right down to the ball, striking it as low as possible, beneath knee height.

OVERHAND SERVE. Meet the ball about a foot over your head, slightly in front of your body. Let the ball roll off your palm to your fingertips. Follow the ball with your eyes *all the time.*

Use your imagination in practicing serves. Mix them up. And when you find a certain serve working well for you, keep practicing it, as you would a stroke, so that its execution becomes, more or less, second nature.

"English," hooks, cuts, slices

Players often inquire about "natural" and "reverse" hops: applying "English" to the ball. In answer, I always say that you must control all other phases of the game before you attempt to put "stuff" on the ball. And, in learning the natural or reverse it should be emphasized that such shots are useless if they cannot be controlled.

The natural hop is executed in the same manner as you would turn a knob to open a door: clockwise with a slight downward twist of the wrist. The ball is met low on its descent at the juncture of the palm and fingers, and then is rolled off the ends of the thumb and first two fingers. In baseball it would be similar to the overhand curve ball.

The reverse hop is an unnatural move, counterclockwise, like the screwball in baseball. The ball is again met low on its descent, with the wrist and hand movement coming down and away from the body. This shot is hard on the arm, for it takes a lot out of it, but many of the top players use it in conjunction with the natural hop to keep the opponent guessing.

Defense for the hops? Don't commit yourself too soon. Let the ball break after it hits the floor and then make your move. Remember, if the ball is hit hard enough to come off a side or back wall before you take it, the "English" will be taken off the ball.

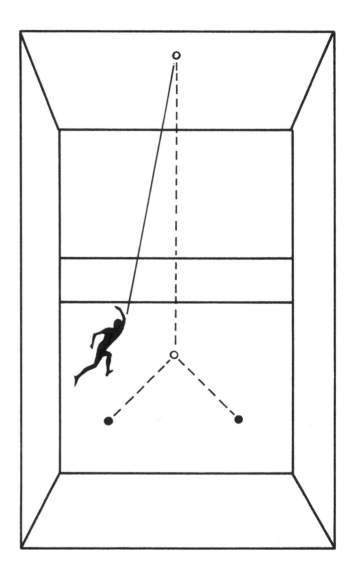

PUTTING "ENGLISH" ON THE BALL. Hooking the ball will make it "break" when it hits the floor.

3

the basic shots

There are three basic shots in handball: the passing shot, the kill shot, and the ceiling shot. Once you've developed a feel for and some skill with the basic strokes (overhand, sidearm, and underhand), start practicing shots with these strokes—put them to use. The handball shots is what you do with them. Practice the shot by yourself—solo—and then put them to use in a game. I'm assuming that by now you are playing fairly regularly (three times a week is usual), but don't on this account give up practicing solo any chance you have. To become a really skillful handball player it is necessary to master the fundamentals so thoroughly you can perform them without thinking. You'll want to have your mind free in a game to use in evaluating your opponent's strengths and weaknesses and to work out a strategy that will make maximum use of your own strengths in order to beat him.

Passing shot

The passing shot is a beautiful thing to see executed, for what it does is outsmart your opponent. If he is in front of you, the idea is to hit the ball to the front wall so that

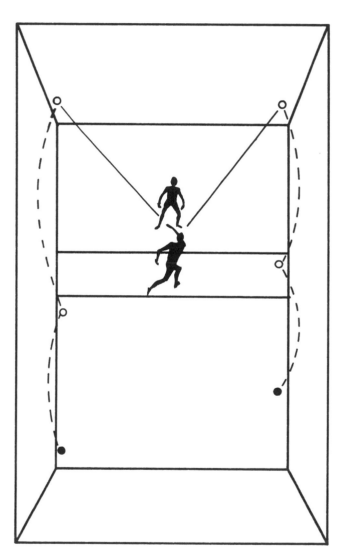

PASSING SHOT. The ball should hug one of the side walls.

it returns out of his reach; that is, it passes him. The passing shot has the considerable merit of making your opponent run and run, and this, of course, tires him.

More often than not, the passing shot is a fast, hard-hit ball, but it can just as well be a "soft" or slow shot, since its objective is solely to give your opponent a ball he will have to chase to return. The passing shot can be hit with any of the three basic strokes—the choice depending on your strengths among the strokes and the game situation—and generally it is hit when your opponent is in the front court or near a side wall. It is most difficult to pass a player who is stationed in midcourt, but it can be done by angling the ball off either side wall, behind your opponent. Keep the ball low, so it won't come off the back wall as a set-up for your opponent.

I've said that the passing shot is *usually* hard hit. Personally, I prefer a softer pass, one that will pass your opponent but not so fast that it will rebound from the back wall with enough force to bring it within playing distance of your opponent. Properly executed in appropriate situations, especially when you feint one way and hit the other, the passing shot will score more points for you than any other shot in your arsenal.

PASSING SHOT IN RIGHT COURT. Use the overhand shot. Meet the ball shoulder high with good velocity. Put the ball down right side. Opponent should be in deep court left or in front court left if a shot from deep court right is to be effective. Vice versa if you are in left court.

Kill shot

While the passing shot should, ordinarily, be the most-used offensive weapon of a handball player, beginners tend to try the kill shot more often. This is understandable —since the kill shot is not only spectacular but, theoretically, also unreturnable—but I'd advise you to spend a good many sessions of practice on your kill before you begin to rely on it for points in a game to the exclusion of other shots.

The classic kill is hit from a crouch, when the ball is close to the floor, and is aimed at the bottom of the front wall. Beginners will often attempt to kill a ball off a high bounce; don't you do it. A kill attempted from a high bounce comes off the front wall at almost the same angle at which it strikes it, leaving your opponent an easy, high-bounce return. Get low, and hit low, and there will be no chance for a return. After a properly executed kill shot the ball will roll out from or come off the front wall with such a low bounce that your opponent can't play it. In either case, the ball has been killed; there is no possibility of a return. But while the kill is handball's most effective shot, the kill is also the hardest to learn. Give it plenty of attention in your practice sessions before you lean on it in game situations.

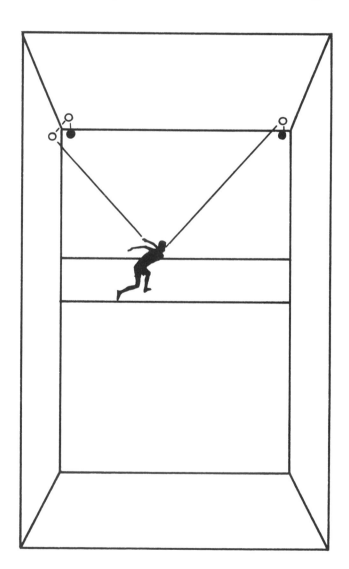

KILL SHOT. Generally the sidearm shot is used. Aim the ball so that it hits the front wall as low as possible.

The most exciting kill shot there is to watch is the one that hits the front wall (or corner) and rolls out, no bounce at all. Usually the kill is made with the sidearm stroke, quite low, as I've said, and very often from off the back wall. The killer thus has the time needed to get into good leg and arm position (that centerline of the body again), and in most cases strokes from somewhere between knee and ankle. (Incidentally, contrary to the recommendations of many other players and teachers, I don't recommend trying for kills directly in front of yourself. If your opponent is anywhere near you and makes an attempt to retrieve, a good referee will call a hinder and your energy—plus the opportunity to put the ball away with some other shot—will have been wasted. If you're playing without a referee, your opponent has every right to demand a hinder if he doesn't have a clear view of the ball as he attempts a return. As you shoot your kills away from your body, your opponent does have an opportunity to retrieve, but by the time he has, if he does, you will be in a commanding offensive position and perhaps can end the rally with your next shot.)

As your game improves, you will learn to hedge your bet on a kill shot by angling it to one of the side walls before it goes to the front wall and dies—or from front wall to side wall for the kill. Such hedging throws your opponent off balance and increases your chances of making the kill and gives you a psychological edge over your opponent that may mean the game, since it demonstrates your control. When you've mastered the shot to your satisfaction, by all means use it. And when you use it—or any other shot from your arsenal—think winning! Thinking you will win, helps.

During the heat of a rally, the good player is always looking for a chance to hit the ball before it reaches the floor—on the volley, as it's called—and to make a kill shot out of the maneuver, if this is possible. Such an on-the-fly shot is called the fly kill. A shot that can be delivered with any of the basic strokes, the fly kill's big advantage is surprise; it is the kind of shot that throws your opponent off balance and draws him out of position. His cerebral computer expects that ball to bounce on the floor and hit a wall or two before you get around to returning it. By rushing forward, or to the side, or backward, and stroking the ball in flight, you unnerve him, at the least, and score on him, in many instances. Watch for potential fly kill shots as your opponent (or you!) starts to tire and the pace of the game and the speed of the ball start to slow down, and the ball begins to bounce higher. Even if you can't convert a fly shot into a kill shot, the fly shot is still an effective offensive weapon.

STRAIGHT KILL IN RIGHT COURT. Level off low, transferring your weight to your front (left) foot. Use sidearm stroke, going for the corner or the front wall near the side wall. Note that your forearm and hand are parallel to floor, meeting ball at the ideal point of contact: away from center of body, knee high, as weight transfers to left foot. Opponent should be in deep court left or in front court left for kill from deep court right to be effective. Vice versa if you are in left court.

RIGHT CORNER KILL WITH LEFT (OFF) HAND.
Lead (right) foot is kept at slight angle to *right* corner as weight shifts. Knees are flexed, and the ball is met away from body, about knee high. The ball comes off your left hand with wrist action as your weight is shifted from your back (left) to your front (right) foot. Your left arm swings across your body. The completion of the swing involves stroking the ball low, with a smooth follow through.

Ceiling shot

The ceiling shot is used defensively by most players. If you should find yourself playing an opponent who relies chiefly, say, on kill shots for his offense, go to the ceiling shot; its high bounce makes it a difficult return to kill. (A caution here, however: improperly executed, the ceiling shot will come off the back wall hard enough to be easily killed.) Use it also to move your opponent out of the front court.

The ceiling shot is hit off the ceiling close to the front wall, usually with an overhand stroke, though it can be hit with an underhand stroke as well.

When you feel you've gained enough experience and skill to try an advanced shot, practice the ceiling shot off your fist, rather than off your palm and fingers. Make a fist with your thumb extended against your index finger (not curled over your fingers) and hit the ball to the ceiling. Such a shot, sometimes called a "bolo," has the advantages of defense and surprise. I use a fist on the ceiling shot when I'm trying to give my opponent a particularly rough return shot—usually down the wall covered by his off

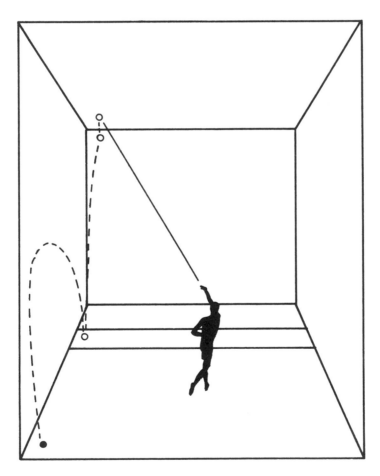

CEILING SHOT. A useful defensive shot. Use an overarm shot to send the ball to the ceiling, then to the front wall, in order to gain time.

arm. To demonstrate this shot—and to teach the photographer for this book, Art Shay, how to play the left-hand corner—I fisted six ceiling shots in a row to the same spot and scored six quick points. (As soon as Shay backed up and waited for the ball to come off the rear wall before trying his return, he stopped being a pigeon.)

Whether you develop a good "fist" variation on your overhand or underhand stroke, however, think of that ceiling as the court's fifth wall, and use it. When you feel yourself tiring and in need of a breather, hit to the ceiling. Those high bounces from the ceiling shot eat up time and give your body a chance to recover from those energy-consuming charges after passing shots and from those mad dashes to the front wall for shots that barely make it off the wall alive.

The effectiveness of the ceiling shot grows in direct proportion to your opponent's inability to handle a high overhand shot with his weak arm, so practice the shot now, at this early stage of your game, and don't always try to pulverize the ball. Instead, as a change of pace (good for you, bad for your opponent), use a light, feather-touch overhand, letting the ball roll from your palm upward off the fingers. Remember, one function of the ceiling shot is to move your opponent out of the front court and give yourself time to take command.

Ideally, the ceiling shot results in a weak return, or even a non-return, by your opponent, who is, if you've gotten off a good shot, plastered up against the rear wall as he makes his own shot, or attempts to. If he gets his shot back to the front wall, you can clobber him somewhere up front with your next one.

CEILING SHOT. Hit the ball when it is about a foot above your head, just in front of your body. "Feather touch" the ball, rolling it from your palm to your fingertips for a shot to the ceiling.

Back-wall shots

Back-wall shots are at first difficult for the beginner because they require experience in angle-judging and moving into proper position to play the ball. Otherwise, the same stroking rules generally apply—that is, hit the ball off that centerline. Many beginners bobble at the back wall because they rush their shots and miss the centerline, sometimes by a couple of feet. Let the ball come to you from the back wall. Don't be afraid to let it fall to knee height before stroking it. Depend on your sidearm mostly for back-wall shots, because the sidearm motion gives your body the best chance of a good retrieve and return, but practice every kind of shot off the back wall—kill, passing, around the wall—and if you've practiced them, don't be hesitant about using them in a game.

Practice session

Whenever you have the opportunity, get into a court and practice the basic strokes and the basic shots—using the basic strokes —by yourself. For short-court shots, throw

The sidearm shot is handball's basic tool. Fast decisions must be made: to play ball off the side or the back wall.

the ball up to the front wall (or front wall, side wall) and move in from *three-quarters court* for the shot. Throw the ball to the back wall and practice back-wall shots. Then stand at the short line and throw the ball into the front wall (or front wall, side wall) and take the ball on the fly. Practice both kills and passing shots. Practice the various serves. Give yourself a workout with a one-man rally, keeping the ball in play against yourself as long as you can. And practice with your off hand, throwing the ball with it and delivering overhand strokes with it. And, as I've said before, when you feel, in practice, that a stroke is working right for you, keep on practicing it. The same holds true for a shot. Try to duplicate it again and again. Master it. This is how you will gain control of your shots, and

I would estimate that winning at handball is 75 percent control. If you don't learn control, you will invariably lose to players who are not as "good" as you are, but who are steadier—who have more control.

In practice, pick out a spot for your shot and come as close to that spot as you possibly can—again and again. Do the same in a game—pick a spot and deliver to it. Be a planner, not a scatter-shot. When you're playing a game and you find that your opponent has fewer skills than you have, give him a handicap of so many points so that you have to press to beat him. Finally, as I suggested earlier, every so often play a game of off hand against off hand. You will find it a very tough game, indeed, but it will do wonders for your off hand—and for your game.

Back-wall play.

Stuffy Singer positions himself defensively for a back wall return.

4

playing to win

By now, with the basic strokes and shots of handball at least rudimentarily learned, you should be practicing or playing at least three times a week—probably playing much more than practicing by now. Don't let yourself slide into an infrequent-playing rut after the first few months of your early enthusiasm. There are many hours in a day; if you can't arrange to take an hour off at lunch for a session on the court, play at night. Force yourself to take the time; make it a habit. You will find that playing handball does not interfere with your work. Quite the contrary, the invigoration and mental and muscular tone you acquire on the handball court will help you in handling your on-the-job problems.

Handball is the cheapest health insurance you can buy, and I firmly believe that a minimum of three sessions a week will provide all the physical outlet and conditioning a person needs. (I'm not the only champion who conditions himself solely through playing the game. Vic Hershkowitz, considered by many the finest all-around player in the history of the game, and a national champion in one-wall, three-wall, and four-wall, has played nothing but handball for exercise for more than 30 years.) But if you positively can't make it to a court at least three times a week, other exercise can help keep you in trim.

Off the court you may well want to supplement your on-court warm-up routine (arm-flailing, kneebends, etc.) with a conditioning regimen that might include swimming, jogging, and push-ups. Touching your toes while seated on the floor and rocking gently forward and back is a good exercise for handball because it loosens up the midsection, making it easier to reach those low shots and to come charging toward the front wall when necessary. If used sparingly, weight lifting can help to build up your power.

The best exercise of all, perhaps, for the handball player is the tried-and-true formula: Pushing away from the groaning, carbohydrate-laden table. Sweet rolls, I think, have destroyed more handball players than every form of business or domestic stress combined. One of the evil traditions of handball—possibly harking back to its New York City childhood—is sweet rolls and coffee after an hour of hard handball. The coffee-klatch discussion often includes self-righteous boasting about weight loss. Not to be self-righteous myself, I recommend the Bob Kendler-inspired custom around USHA headquarters—hot soup after a game. (Speaking of weight loss, I've often lost as much as 15 pounds in a four-day tournament. Somehow, though, it is possible to find liquids to replenish the loss.)

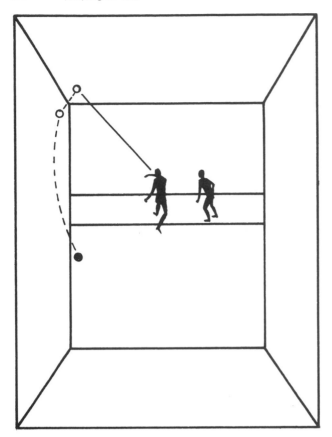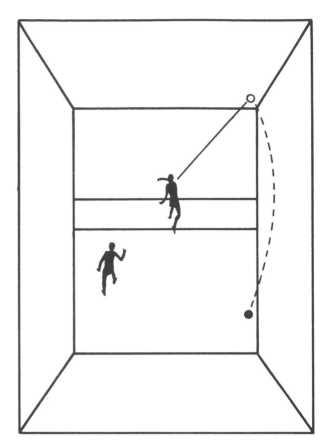

GOOD OFFENSIVE PLAY. The player who dominates center court can use his position to great advantage.

So much for the physical conditioning needed to win. On the court, after you have mastered the fundamentals and have a knowledge of when to use your offense and when to use your defense, you are—like any other combat unit—ready to concentrate on how to get to 21 first. Handball is, among many other things, a game of rallies. You hit the ball and your opponent returns it, your objective being to hit the ball so that he can't return it. Your objective, then, is to end the rally, and the secret of doing this is to hit the very best shot you can to your opponent's absolute weakest area.

As your arsenal of fundamental shots comes more and more under your control (that's to say, as you are more and more able to hit the ball where you want to hit it), the cerebral aspects of the game will begin to bring home points, if you master

them. You must learn to out-think and out-diagnose your opponents as well as out-shoot them. You are your own quarterback, offense, defense—and rooting section!

There are many rally-ending shots: a good kill shot from front or deep court, passing shots down either wall, fly shots that pass or are kills—but the important thing is to know when to use each of them. During the course of a rally you will often find your opponent in deep court after retrieving a defensive return, for example. If you can command center-court position at the short line, attempt a kill shot in such a situation, either in the corner or straight to the front wall. It won't be necessary to hit the front wall within an inch of the floor to score a kill; within a foot or so will do for this kill, because your opponent is well behind you.

To take another example, say that both you and your opponent are in front court and you have the opportunity to take the ball out of the air on the volley and surprise him. In such a situation, it would be wise to try to make the ball pass him down one side or the other. Enough such passing shots and you will run him right into the floor, especially if it's late in the game.

There are other elements to winning, among them anticipation, concentration, control. Let's start with anticipation.

Anticipation

Constructive anticipation is one of the most difficult aspects of the game for the beginning handball player to develop. There seems more than enough to do just getting into position and making a return, much less trying to anticipate what kind of shot your opponent is going to counter with. But as you gain control of your own game, and experience from playing, you will be able— by studying your opponent's style, by listening to him as he moves about the court, by watching him as he sets himself to stroke— to anticipate with reasonable accuracy what kind of shot is coming back at you. (*Reasonable* accuracy; your opponent, of course, is trying to anticipate what you may be anticipating, and therefore he will . . . etc. Not surprisingly if you think about it, it is often harder to anticipate what a beginning player may shoot than an experienced player, since the beginner not only often does not counter with the logical shot for a given situation, but in many instances misfires when he does respond logically.)

Suppose, however, that your relatively untutored opponent is swinging from the left side of the court. He will almost always then hit the ball to the right side of the court (and vice versa), since his body has fallen into good position for returning the ball to the opposite court. Determine early in the game his favorite shots; they will probably be made by him as often as he has oppor-

tunity; stay back and wait for them. By closely observing his style of play, and his strengths and weaknesses, you will eventually be able to anticipate where he is going to hit the ball. And gradually you will begin —consciously and unconsciously—to take advantage of this foreknowledge and move sure-footedly into good position for your return shots. The good player arrives at the "right spot" a little early, giving him ample time to set himself for his next shot.

Handball, like chess and war, consists of offense and defense. When you have the serve and are trying to score points, you are on the offense. When your opponent is sniping at you with his offensive weapons on his serve, you of course are on the defense. But even when you are server and technically on the offense, you will often find yourself making defensive shots. These will be shots that you can just barely retrieve, or shots that you must make from poor position, or returns of near-kill shots that you just manage to get to. Thus, each time that you stroke the ball you are making either an offensive or a defensive shot, and the seemingly automatic decision of which shot it will be will be made instinctively. How is this instinct developed?

By practice. Game practice and solo practice. Practice in observing other players in a game, practice in observing your opponents as they play you, practice in observing the flight of the ball around the court. But even when a beginning player has honed his anticipation skills to a fine, cutting edge, he will often have a tendency to rush the ball as it comes to him and to swing too soon. I caution you: Wait. Get your body set; let the ball hit the imaginary centerline before you stroke it; make your shot with all of your body in controllable position. With control you can almost always make those point-scoring offensive shots. With control *and* anticipation, you'll be a tournament player in no time—or in very little time, at any rate.

Concentration

Baseball is invariably described as a game of inches. A quarter of an inch difference in the position of ball on bat is the difference between a home run and a weak pop fly; an inch to the right and that foul ball is fair; and so forth. So it is with handball: most of the games you play will be decided by a matter of "inches" difference between you and your opponent. Anticipation is one means of gaining those precious inches for yourself; concentration is another.

In a recent national tournament I could sense my opponent's tenseness at a particular point in the game. (You will gradually learn to "read" your opponent's frame of mind the way good poker players read mental sets at the table.) So instead of using the hard, driving serve he was expecting, because I had been using it, I changed to a lob. He was so concerned about whether the ball would break left or right, he gave me an easy point. He had momentarily ceased to concentrate on the actual shot that was coming to him—one that in ordinary circumstances he could easily have returned—and instead had let his tenseness take over.

Handball is the kind of sport that forces you to concentrate on what is happening *now*, if you expect to stay in that particular game. If your mind wanders off the court to ponder a business problem, or starts to work up a better answer to your wife than you actually made before gym time, you're quickly a pigeon on that court. The same holds true if, say, you should start hitting the ball and making believe it's the business competitor who's causing that problem (or, God forbid, your wife). The activity may be good for your psyche and give healthful release to all kinds of pent-up aggressions, but the result is bad handball.

Your mental approach to a game should be one of forced, determined calm and concentration. I like to think of waiting for an opponent's serve as just as mind clearing as the Yoga technique of imagining yourself in a long, dark tunnel concentrating on a lit candle at the far end of the tunnel. If you are concentrating properly on a handball court, the only job you have in the world is to return that little black ball in such a way and to such a point that your opponent will not be able to return it to you.

A psychiatrist I know, who is a first-rate handball player, says that handball has kept him off the couch himself: "It lets me get rid of my aggressions and frustrations without naming them. The sense of achievement that winning handball gives a man is priceless. It follows in line from our tribal beginnings. It is still important for man to triumph physically. Sports is just about all that's left where he can do that, and for me, handball works best."

I agree, but I know he isn't thinking about any of that while he's on the court, or he wouldn't be a first-rate player; he's thinking about returning that little black ball where I can't get to it.

Control

I am assuming that you have been practicing and developing your game at a heartening pace and that you are serious about moving up the handball ladder. Inevitably, this brings up the matter of control. Control is what separates the duffers from the players, and right about now you should be ready for a strong dose of control therapy. Your game should be refining itself to where you can place the ball pretty much where you want it, controlling the ball's movement both offensively and defensively—speed and direction. That is control—but there are other elements involved in control, too, and I can speak on the subject because I learned the hard way.

UNDERHAND FIST STROKE WITH LEFT (OFF) HAND. Facing the side wall, move your front (right) foot toward ball, shifting your weight to that foot. Uppercut. Ball goes to ceiling. The off-hand fist follows through toward the ceiling.

As I said, I began to play handball at a very early age. It wasn't until I was in my late twenties, however, that I began to win the big state and national tournaments. What was wrong with my game—or me—during my early twenties, the time when most good handball players develop? It took me many, many matches to identify my problem: I was not in control of my game. I was hitting and returning by guess and by gosh all over the court, street style.

One way I'd lose control—and, oh, how many ways there are!—was with my chronic case of the dives. I would dive for almost every low ball that came within diving range. This would occasionally give me some spectacular returns, but more often it would leave me with skinned knees flat on the floor while my opponent passed balls around one side or the other. It took me a long time to discover that you can actually reach a low ball faster and more efficiently —with control—by getting low, flexing those knees, and returning, and that by going after them like that you maintain position to stay in the rally.

Another game-control problem I had to lick was my tendency to play offense when I should have been on defense. That fault cost me quite a few tournaments. To overcome it, I developed that feather-touch ceiling shot with either hand I've mentioned. (I've even begun to use this defensive ploy as an offensive weapon, running my opponents into the deep corners with it.)

Control can be valued at as much as 75 percent of your game once you've mastered the physical fundamentals. Control your shots. Control the ball. Most important of all, control your emotions! When you miss a shot, don't get angry at yourself. Just resolve to make the next shot. Self-anger is one of the most destructive opponents you will meet on the court. When you flub a shot, simply grit your teeth and carry on.

Loosen your arms, flex your knees, get ready to make the next one. After all, it's only—ha, ha—a game. (Around the Northwest YMCA in Des Plaines, Illinois, one of the gentlest and most affable men in the world, Mike Hecht, has given his name to the handball world as a synonym for a missed or bobbled shot. Each time Mike misses, his anger at himself spurts out the most shocking expletive he can bring himself to utter: "Mike *HECHT!* Mike *HECHT!*" This terrible curse sounds so much better than the others commonly used

EYE ON BALL. Follow the ball with your eyes right into the glove and out again.

for self-anger that everyone now uses it.)

Part and parcel of good control is, of all things, patience. Wait for good opportunities. Don't force the play and risk making shots from unprepared positions. Don't aim helter-skelter. Don't depend on your off hand as an offensive weapon, since this often results in overswinging, bobbles, and loss of control. If your opponent gets a lead, don't panic. Stay with your fundamentals and let your opponent make errors. Invariably when faced with a good, steady, fundamental player, opponents do make those errors; their concentration lapses, and they begin thinking, "Won't this guy ever miss?" and they miss.

Another, seemingly obvious, aspect of control is: Watch the ball. A sportswriter once made a joke, saying, "Haber even keeps his eye on the ball during time-outs." You know something? I do. *Never* take your eye off the ball. Follow it right into the hand—into your own hand and into your opponent's hand.

Court strategy

Overall, your game should be keyed to your physical makeup. If you are in good shape and can run like a deer, develop a running game that permits you to rally your opponent into a perspiring heap. Keep the ball away from him with high lobs and back-court and ceiling shots. Take advantage of these tactics if you can master them.

If you are a bull and have power (under control—always under control!), don't hesitate to powder the ball every chance you have. When the opportunity presents itself, surprise your opponent with a wickedly hard shot that he either can't reach or can't handle because of its force.

Some players win matches by wearing their opponents down, taking advantage of

errors and, finally, thoroughly exasperating a player who appears to be a better-hitting, power player.

Some players develop a good, big serve and an acceptable kill shot. These can carry them into tournaments, but rarely all the way to the top, since such players rarely have the stamina for long rallies, and, moreover, their strategy is so obvious it can readily be nullified by a good player who has a more rounded arsenal at his command.

If you are in good shape—or at least better shape than your opponent—I recommend that in addition to running like a deer you alternate your returns so that your opponent has the farthest possible distance to cover in returning. One of the mysteries of handball to me is how many beginners and intermediate players almost compulsively return their shots direct to their opponents. Some of them, if they tried to be as accurate as they are, couldn't do it, but there they are, right to the mark each shot. Make believe you're a big league pitcher and mix 'em up. (One of the best pick-up handball games I ever watched was between former big league pitchers Jim Brosnan and Jay Hook. They psyched either other up and down the court; there was absolutely no pattern to their play, so resolutely were they mixing 'em up.)

In the course of a rally, when your opponent is in front of you, resist the temptation to kill the ball. Think, rather, of passing him with a shot. Only think of a kill if your adversary is alongside of you or, preferably, behind you. There will be exceptions to this rule, of course, but I'm speaking of the percentages.

Occasionally during a rally you may see an opening for a kill but find yourself out of position for an eventual return should you miss with the kill attempt. In such a case, I recommend a safe, high ceiling shot rather than the off-balance try for the kill. The long-run percentages of handball play dictate this kind of safe-playing over chance-taking. I'm not knocking the great off-balance kills and spectacular retrieves we've all seen (and in some cases made), but if your interest is in becoming a gradually improving tournament player, stick with the percentages. For the beginner I'd recommend trying the kill only when he is 100 percent in balance from beginning to end of shot.

Patience soon becomes a function of control as well as strategy. Wait for your openings. Get set properly whenever you can. The good hunter patiently stalks his kill.

5

game plans

As early as possible in your handball career you should start planning your games. (When a sportswriter asks me, "Did the game go according to your game plan?" I know he is one of the few sportswriters who really understand handball.) Begin with your capabilities. You know how good or bad your off hand is; you know if that twisted ankle is strong enough for charges to the front wall. And, of course, calculate your opponent's capabilities. Does he have a "spare tire" that will slow him down or does he look like a born miler? If you've seen him play before, perhaps you concluded he warms up slowly. If this is so, your game plan might include trying for short rallies and quick kills and shots into the corners to keep him from warming up on your time, and to score a lot of points before he's actually physically ready to play his best game.

Or say that your opponent's off hand appears to be especially weak in his warm-up. Resolve, then, to hit to that weakness whenever possible. Or say that you watch him misjudge a back-wall ball by two feet during warm-up. Make sure that when the game starts you give him plenty of back-wall shots to worry about. This is war! And the idea is to *win!*

Of course your opponent will be sizing you up at the same time you are studying him, and he will have formulated a game plan of his own. Perhaps he will think you are a little short-winded, and he may, because of this, be planning to hit the ball away from you the first game, to keep you running back and forth.

If you perceive his game plan, why not alter your own game plan and race in for fly kills, or shoot for the corners, giving him little time to get set for lobs that will run you?

Then, of course, he may get wise to your game plan's alteration and alter his own plan. It sounds complicated, but it's only common sense at work, and it's fun.

You must always call defensive signals for yourself as well as offensive, and you must be loose enough and limber enough— mentally as well as physically—to alter those signals when alteration is necessary. It makes a surprisingly cerebral game of a sport that looks, to outsiders, like a ballet exercise performed by hard-running, hard-sweating brutes.

Suppose you run up against a power hitter. On their home courts, power hitters often have just enough stuff to win. At a tournament of good players, however, they are soon sitting in the gallery wondering how they got beaten. Well, the simplest way to beat a power hitter is to neutralize his power with shots that keep him in the back court, from where the percentage of his successful kill shots will go down drastically. In addition, the blasters are so accustomed to ending rallies quickly that they are not geared to playing long games and will often tire. The trick is to move them around the court by hitting away from them and making them run long and hard for retrieves.

I've beaten hard-hitting Bill Yambrick of St. Paul three times for national championships because, against me, he doggedly stays with a volleying game. Bill has won other championships from good opponents with this type of game, but somehow I have been able to break through it and play my own game plan to beat him. The anti-Yambrick game plan is simple: I shoot for more kills than I would against a less talented player. Bill has an excellent off hand, but I think he overuses it, providing me with too many offensive openings during key periods of tournament games. It seems obvious to me that Bill should change his strategy against me, but after all these years it seems unlikely that he will. . . . Of course he may read this and I'll be a dead duck next time we play!

Tempo, momentum, percentages

There is rhythm and tempo to victory and defeat. In a basketball game one team is behind, gets hot, starts hitting its shots, and ties the score. The whistle blows. The coach victimized by the hot streak—the momentum toward victory—has called time out. He is trying to cool down his team's oppressors and, on the offensive side, psych up his own team into a winning tempo and momentum. Sometimes it works; sometimes it doesn't.

Time outs can be used profitably in handball, too. You are allowed three 30-second time outs during each game. If you're feeling okay, have a lead, and have good momentum, there's no need to call a time out. However, if you fall behind, call time and try to analyze your predicament. Try to discover what's going wrong. Do this as soon as possible. It's the first step toward a cure.

When you are ahead, my advice to you is: *Never let up!* Be a "nice guy" after you win, not during a match.

When you start playing tournaments, do as the operating surgeon does—get in and get out as quickly as possible. That is, get

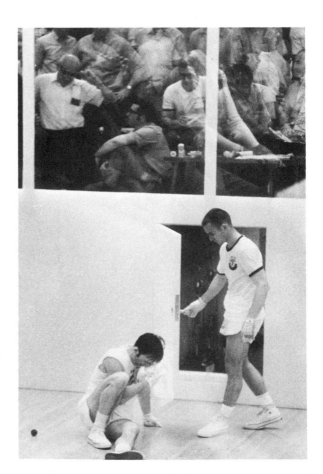

TIME OUT!

on the court, start the game, keep a fast tempo, try to build up a big lead, and never let up. Get into the winning groove immediately, and stay there. Think of yourself as a winner and you are a long way down the path toward winning. (Any high school or college athlete will be reminded by these words of his various coaches spurring him on. It's good psychology, necessary, and often works. There are very few "cold" champions.)

Never let up. Too often I've seen players almost literally blast their opponents off the court for 10 or 15 points, then—figuring they can take it easy for a few points—relax. Before they can regain their momentum, they've lost the game.

As in any other sport, there are definite percentages in handball. The odds for and against certain shots in certain situations can be computed—and you will be roughly computing them as you gain experience—and players like to talk about the value of certain shots as opposed to others. For example, if a player tries to shoot offensively from deep court time after time, he will find himself making errors or setting up easy shots for his opponent. So, bad odds on such shots. It happens, of course, that a player can have a hot streak and rack up a string of points with such bad-percentage tactics, but a full match usually serves as an equalizer. That's one of the fascinations of handball: you can have a bad streak, even lose badly; but in a best-of-three-game match, you have every opportunity to dig in and make a comeback from far behind.

The important thing is not to get flustered if your game plan doesn't immediately work. Be patient. I have seen a player using the lob serve get behind 14-1, but stick with the serve and eventually win when, as the player had calculated his opponent would, his opponent began making errors.

Learn which shots you can make with the most consistency, and learn the court positions from which you excel. Say that for you, in emergency situations—retrieving a shot to the back wall in your strong-hand corner, for example—the percentages dictate a sidearm shot to the opposite front corner. All right—make that shot. Don't try an overhand if your overhand has been untrustworthy. Bet on yourself; learn your best percentages, that is, how to play so that you stand a good chance of pulling off the shot you attempt, and play them and the odds on your victories will improve.

As a general rule, I'd suggest that if you are able to return the ball with your strong hand and the shot is below waist level and you aren't more than 30 feet from the front wall, try an offensive shot. Be aggressive and the odds on your victories will also improve.

It is very important to remember with the percentage shots that you can risk more when you are serving than when you are receiving. When you are the server and go for the kill and miss, you don't lose a point, but when you are the receiver and miss, your opponent posts a big point. There are many handballers who thought that Oscar Obert, a two-time national four-wall singles champion and winner of many state and regional honors, was too reckless in his shooting. Closer observation would have shown them that Oscar took most of his go-for-broke deep-court fly and straight kill attempts when he was in service. On the receiving end he played a much safer game and worked to get the serve back.

By concentrating on your game you will avoid falling into set patterns that enable your opponent to anticipate your moves. As I've said, mix up your offense. Even though you have an excellent right-corner kill, you'll find your opponent moving in quickly if you continually use it. Keep him honest by shooting occasional passes to his left, a straight left-corner kill. He'll get the message. On deep-court returns, if you find your opponent lagging in back court with you, switch from defense to offense and fire in a safe kill. By "safe kill" I mean a corner or straight shot not aimed at that bottom board but low enough so your man can't move to front court in time to retrieve it. The percentage of the safe kill success is high, and you can't hurt yourself using it.

Doubles play

By now the chances are that some of your practice has been accomplished with three other players on the court, and you have tasted the glories and frustrations of doubles play. There is really no set pattern for good doubles play—except load-sharing—but there are a few generalities that may be useful to you. If two righthanders pair up, it is usually understood that the man playing the left side will dominate the play. The chief reason for this is that his strong hand will cover the center of the court, where the traffic is heaviest. The other man subordinates his play, keeps the opposing team on the defensive, and sets up situations that his partner can convert into points.

Teamwork, of course, is the essence of doubles play. Two good singles players will

DOUBLES. Note the concentration of the players. The three players not actually playing the ball stand ready, feet forward, for the return.

not necessarily beat a team that they have beaten man for man in singles; on the contrary, two fair players who team well together can often clobber two superior singles who do not play as a cohesive team. Choose your doubles partner to complement your own style. A doubles player who's a good shotmaker and who has quick hands should make a good short-cut, up-front man when teamed with a deep, booming-shot player who is at home off the ceiling or back wall.

The right side is not as easy to play as it might at first seem to be, however. Not only must that player be content to play second fiddle, but he must also be ready to retrieve low, driving shots, move quickly to deep court—and know which shots to let go. Too many right-side players will "stick out their left hand" when the shot should be taken by their partner's strong right hand. The ego is involved in handball, and doubles play somehow injures a few egos. The right-side player (whatever his ego involvement) must not let himself be caught playing too close to the right wall, for then he will be forced to use his off hand.

In everyday "club" play, the usual procedure is to alternate serves in doubles, first to one opponent, then to the other. This gives all players a good workout and is regarded as good sportsmanship. In tournament play, however, the objective is to ferret out the weaker partner, and more specifically his weak arm, and keep hitting to that, serve after serve, shot after shot.

When a lefthander and a righthander team up, the pattern is changed. The middle-court area is now most vulnerable, and the two must coordinate properly to let the man in the better position take center-court balls. Since the two side alleys are well protected by such a combination, more knowledgeable opponents will use many front-wall, side-wall shots together with straight-down-the-middle shots that are low and driving.

Doubles can be very enjoyable, for the game presents the challenge of teamwork (without the regimentation of large-team organization), the necessity of pinpoint control (since you are shooting against two possible retrievers), and it is also somewhat less energy-draining than singles play. It has the disadvantage of the possibility of an excessive number of hinder calls.

Tournament play

Don't pace yourself in your early tournament play. Condition yourself for three or more grueling days of hard handball and go all out from the very first game.

Surprised by such advice? It's the best that I can give you, because no matter how much hometown Y or club competition you have beaten, there is no comparison between it and the tournament pressures you will meet in playing against styles that have won in various parts of the country.

You'll find the old adrenalin pumping faster from the beginning, so don't be surprised if you get that exhausted, played-out feeling after the very first game. If you're in any kind of shape—and you should be if you intend to enter tournaments—your second wind will come and you will bounce back quickly. Gulp in all the air you can when you feel tired. The oxygen snaps you back.

I find that most players in tournaments get arm weary by the time they reach the finals—if they reach the finals. They use so much power on their serves and rallies that their strong arm ends up aching. Practice the use of the lob serve. The ability to use it will come in handy when you need it most.

Before a tournament I condition myself

In handball your back is often to the wall—and some-times, so is your head!

by playing hours and hours of handball against any kind of competition available. To keep a sharp, competitive edge, I often take on two opponents at the same time, allowing them points to force myself to play hard. They may not admit it, but I clobbered my collaborators on this book, Mort Leve and Art Shay, this way while preparing for this year's Nationals. I find that long sessions of play sharpen my control, and in the final analysis, as I've stated earlier, it is control that wins games.

Bring along at least one extra pair of gloves to a tournament, and a spare uniform. Four spare T-shirts are not too many. It is much easier to play well if you can change into dry playing clothes and gloves between games. If the court temperature is high and the air is humid because of a packed gallery, you will perspire more than usual and will want a change of gloves and shirt close at hand. Keep your gloves from stiffening by hooking them to the outside of your gym bag where they can "breathe."

Even if you lose in tournament play, you can score a few points for your side by carefully observing the better players. Many championship-caliber players have a pet shot. If any of these strike you as being worthy of adding to your own arsenal, watch the guy as he uses it. Talk to him about it if possible. (At tournaments I'm usually cornered by young players interested in my lob serve and ceiling shots.)

Tournaments are good places to learn what *not* to do, as well. Watch the young power hitters who smoke the ball all over the court. They never make it to the finals, because they can't control those bullets and, thus, they often set up a more experienced player who then runs them off the court with softer, but more strategic, placement.

The complete game in handball has four aspects: power, control, stamina, and speed. I can think of only one player who can be said to have possessed a complete game: Jim Jacobs. Jim won six national singles titles and the same number of national doubles, and would have won more had he not been handicapped by a series of injuries. Fortunately, my prime years have come after his prime, though I did have one moment of glory in winning over him in a highly publicized exhibition on his home court in New York City. Before playing Jacobs, I analyzed the game plan thoroughly. I knew there were at least two areas where he could overshadow me: he could hit the ball harder and he could throw more hooks. So I decided my best chance would be to gamble with the shooting percentages and match my control against his. I was able to win a grueling three-game match because of a good percentage of kills and because of control that enabled me to move him around. Jim became leg-weary in the third game, had to take time out with cramps, and I went on to win the game by a wide margin.

But there is a vast difference between a one-time exhibition match and a week-long national tournament. In the big tournaments the draw can have a significant bearing on the ultimate outcome; if a player can breeze through two-game matches in the early rounds he will be fresher and readier for final-round play than an opponent who has been struggling to keep alive.

I have found, too, that competing in singles *and* in doubles in the same tournament is foolhardy. It simply takes too much out of a player and jeopardizes his chances of winning at either.

During a tournament I try to arrange my days into a reasonable program with lots of rest and not much eating. I never eat a heavy meal within several hours of a match. If I'm scheduled to play in the afternoon or evening, I may start the day with a big breakfast—the old Australian one of steak and eggs—and this will maintain me until after the match.

If I am scheduled to play twice in the same day, I eat well in advance of the first game and then try to get some sleep between the games, and to replenish my dehydrated system with liquids. During a match I have found Gatorade excellent for balancing the loss of body fluid through perspiration. (Don't, incidentally, gulp down ice-cold drinks between games or immediately after a match. Give yourself time to cool off and relax first.)

Saunas and steambaths, if available, can keep you from stiffening up and relax you for your next match. If you come up with any one of the assorted physical injuries that can work against your game, don't neglect it. Get the best help you can—immediately. If you've got a slightly pulled leg muscle, get it wrapped by a trainer. Use the whirlpool bath and massage table for muscle soreness. To protect bone bruises of the palms, apply a Scholl pad or a small pad of foam rubber over the sore spot and pull your glove over it.

Don't be foolhardy and play with an untreated or untreatable injury. You'll be doing yourself a disservice in the long run, if you try to. I made this kind of mistake in 1968. I suffered a torn stomach muscle two weeks before the '68 Nationals, took painkiller shots, and tried to compete. I found myself playing at only about 50 percent of my handball capability. Moreover, the pain returned in the middle of a match. I staggered through to the quarter-finals before losing, but it really wasn't worth the anguish. Respect your body. It's carrying you

through life as well as through handball.

Most tournament players advise against trying for the seemingly impossible retrieve—and so do I, for the most part, if it is really an impossible percentage shot. The theory is that trying for the seemingly impossible retrieve takes too much out of you even if you do return the ball, so that even if you do, the return provides your opponent with a set-up. I have found that by returning one of those seemingly impossible retrieves and keeping the ball in play and then ultimately winning the rally, psychologically I have won a great deal more than just the point or serve; I have, with that retrieve, often won the winning momentum in the game. I like to imagine my opponent thinking: "Here I pound in my best shot and he digs it up. How will I be able to beat him?" Handball is a "psych" sport, and you've got to get the psych working for you.

After a match is over, win or lose, look back on it and make mental notes of what you could have done that would have improved your performance. If you lost, figure out why and what you can do next time to win, or at the least, do better. Aspire to do better. Play and practice yourself through the kind of situations you bobbled in a losing game. Championship means perfection. Perfect yourself. Mend your errors and build on your strong points.

Beneath the championship level are many, many levels of competition—B and C tournaments with small trophies, but big memories—and just plain old handball, hand to hand. Whether you play for fun, conditioning, or trophies, your skills and enjoyment will increase if you play as if there were no substitute for winning.

Chief Judge Bob Kendler, head of USHA, explains the rules to Bill Yambrick and Paul Haber before the championship in Texas.

After a hard-fought victory, Paul Haber accepts congratulations. In the background is the trophy he has just won.

the united states handball association

In 1950 a group of leading handball players and administrators got together to form a players' fraternity. Pioneering the movement was Bob Kendler, who was determined to give the game an individual identity, improve tournament conditions, and standardize court sizes and rules.

Kendler has been head of the USHA during a period of great progress. The association has more than 10,000 members throughout the nation, Canada, Mexico, Ireland, and in many other foreign countries, wherever there are handball courts. The Skokie, Illinois, headquarters is a general clearing house for the game, providing court specifications and instructional and championship play films, publishing a bi-monthly magazine, *Ace*, devoted entirely to handball, and blueprinting plans for state, regional, and national tournaments.

official united states handball association four-wall handball rules

Part I. The Game

Rule 1.1 Types of Games. Four-wall handball may be played by two or four players. When played by two it is called "singles"; when played by four, "doubles."

Rule 1.2 Description. Handball, as the name implies, is a competitive game in which either hand or fist may be used to serve and return the ball.

Rule 1.3 Objective. The objective is to win each volley by serving or returning the ball so that the opponent is unable to keep the ball in play. A serve or volley is won when a side is unable to return the ball before it touches the floor twice.

Rule 1.4 Points and Outs. Points are scored only by the serving side when it serves an ace or wins a volley. When the serving side loses a volley, it loses the serve. Losing the serve is called an "out" in singles, a "hand-out" in doubles.

Rule 1.5 Game. A game is won by the side first scoring 21 points.

Rule 1.6 Match. A match is won by the side first winning 2 games.

Part II. Court and Equipment

Rule 2.1 Court. The specifications for the standard four-wall handball court are:

(a) Dimensions. 20 feet wide, 20 feet high, and 40 feet long, with back wall at recommended height of 12 feet.

(b) Lines and Zones. Handball courts are divided and marked on the floors with 1½-inch-wide red lines as follows:

(1) Short Line. The short line is midway between and parallel to the front and back walls and divides the court into equal front and back courts.

(2) Service Line. The service line is parallel to and located 5 feet in front of the short line.

(3) Service Zone. The service zone is the space between the outer edges of the short and service lines.

(4) Services Boxes. A service box is located at each end of the service zone and is set off by lines 18 inches from' and parallel to each side wall.

(5) Receiving Lines. Five feet back of the short line, vertical lines are marked on each side wall extending 3 inches from the floor. See rule 4.7 (a).

Rule 2.2 Ball Specifications. The specifications for the standard handball are: material, rubber; color, black; size, 1⅞-inch diameter, with ⅟₃₂-inch variation; weight, 2.3 ounces, with a variation of 0.2 ounce; rebound from 70-inch drop: 42–48 inches at a temperature of 68 degrees Fahrenheit.

Rule 2.3 Ball Selection. A new ball is selected by the referee for use in each match in all tournaments. During a game the referee has the authority to change balls if he deems it necessary. The Spalding ACE handball is official for all United States Handball Association-sanctioned tournaments.

Rule 2.4 Gloves. Handball may not be played barehanded. Gloves must be worn. Gloves must be light in color and made of a soft material or leather, and form fitting. The fingers of the gloves may not be webbed or connected or removed. No foreign substance, tape, or rubber hands may be used on the fingers or on the palms of the gloves. No metal or hard substance may be worn on the hand under the glove. For sensitive, bruised, or sore hands surgical gauze or tape may be wrapped around the palm of the hand, with or without foam rubber, for protective purposes. The gloves must be changed when they become so wet that they moisten the ball. Players should have extra dry gloves for each match.

Rule 2.5 Uniform. All parts of the uniform, consisting of a shirt, shorts, socks, and shoes, must be clean. Two basic colors have been added to white as allowable for USHA competition — Columbia Blue (powder blue) and Bright Yellow. These colors can be used in any combination in the shirt, shorts, and socks and are compatible with the SARANAC S-102 color-backed gloves. Only club insignia, name of club, handball organization or sponsoring organization may be on uniform. Players may not play without shirts.

Part III. Officiating

Rule 3.1 Tournaments. All tournaments are managed by a committee or chairman, who designates the officials.

Rule 3.2 Officials. The officials include a referee and a scorer, if available. Additional assistants and record keepers may be designated.

Rule 3.3 Qualifications. Since the quality of the officiating often determines the success of each tournament, all officials must be experienced or trained and must be thoroughly familiar with these rules and with local playing conditions. One of the most important jobs at a tournament is that of "floor manager." The floor manager oversees assignment of referees, readies players for their court assignments, and in general is responsible for the continued progress of the play schedule.

Rule 3.4 Rules Briefing. Before all tournaments, all officials and players must be briefed on rules and on local court hinders or other regulations.

Rule 3.5 Referees.

(a) Pre-match Duties. Before each match commences, it is the duty of the referee to:

(1) Check on adequacy of preparation of the handball court with respect to cleanliness, lighting, and temperature, and on location of locker rooms, drinking fountains, etc.

(2) Check on availability and suitability of all materials necessary for the match, including handballs, towels, score cards, and pencils.

(3) Check readiness and qualifications of assisting officials.

(4) Explain court regulations to players and inspect the players for compliance with glove and hand rules. See Rule 2.4.

(5) Remind players to have an adequate supply of extra gloves and shirts.

(6) Introduce players, toss coin to determine order of serve, and signal start of first game.

(b) Decisions. During games the referee decides all questions that may arise in accordance with these rules. If there is body contact on the back swing, the player must call it quickly. This is the only call a player may make. See Rule 4.10 (b). On all questions involving judgment and on all questions not covered by these rules, the decision of the referee is final.

(c) Protests. Any decision not involving the judgment of the referee is, on protest, decided by the tournament chairman, if present, or his delegated representative.

(d) Match Forfeitures. A match is forfeited by the referee when:

(1) Any player refuses to abide by the referee's decision or engages in unsportsmanlike conduct.

(2) Any player leaves the court during a game without permission of the referee.

(3) Any player for a singles match, or any team for a doubles match, fails to report to play. Normally, 20 minutes from the scheduled game time is allowed before forfeiture. The tournament chairman may permit a longer delay if circumstances warrant such a decision.

(e) Rating Forfeitures. If both players for singles, or both teams for doubles, fail to appear to play for consolation matches or other playoffs, they shall forfeit their ratings for future tournaments and forfeit any trophies, medals, or awards. See Rule 5.4.

Note: A forfeiture of a match is the least desirable course of action. Common sense and flexibility are part and parcel of the Players' Fraternity. A referee should not be hasty in any such decision and should retain his composure at all times.

Rule 3.6 Scorers. The scorer keeps a record of the progress of the game in the manner prescribed by the committee or chairman. As a minimum, the progress record must include the order of serves, outs, and points. The referee or scorer must announce the score before each serve.

Rule 3.7 Record Keepers. In addition to the scorer, the committee may designate additional persons to keep more detailed records, for statistical purposes, of the progress of the game.

Part IV. Play Regulations

Rule 4.1 Serve (Generally)
(a) Order. The player or side winning the toss becomes the first server and starts the first game, and the third game, if necessary.
(b) Start. Games are started by the referee calling, "Play ball."
(c) Place. The server may serve from any place in the service zone. No part of either foot may extend beyond either line of the service zone. Stepping on the line (but not beyond it) is permitted. Server must remain in the service zone until the served ball passes short line. Violations are called "foot faults." See Rule 4.5 (a) (1).
(d) Manner. A serve is commenced by bouncing the ball to the floor in the service zone. On the first bounce the ball must be struck by the server's hand or fist so that it hits the front wall and on the rebound hits the floor back of the short line, either with or without touching one of the side walls.
(e) Readiness. Serves may not be made until the receiving side is ready or the referee has called, "Play ball."

Rule 4.2 Serve (In Doubles)
(a) Server. At the beginning of each game in doubles, each side informs the referee of the order of service, which order must be followed throughout the game. Only the first server may serve the first time up and continue to serve first throughout the game. When the first server is out, the side is out. Thereafter, both players on each side serve until a hand-out occurs. It is not necessary for the server to alternate serves to his team's opponents.
(b) Partner's Position. On each serve, the server's partner must stand erect with his back to the side wall and with both feet on the floor within the service box until the served ball passes the short line. Violations are called "foot faults." See Rule 4.5 (a) (2).

Rule 4.3 Defective Serves. Defective serves are of three types resulting in penalties as follows:
(a) Dead-Ball Serve. A dead-ball serve results in no penalty and the server is given another serve without canceling a prior illegal serve. See Rule 4.4.
(b) Fault Serve. Two fault serves result in a hand-out. See Rule 4.5.

(c) Out Serves. An out serve results in a hand-out. See Rule 4-6.

Rule 4.4 Dead-Ball Serves. Dead-ball serves do not cancel any previous illegal serve. They occur when an otherwise legal serve:

(a) Hits Partner. Hits the server's partner on the fly on the rebound from the front wall while the server's partner is in the service box. Any serve that touches the floor before hitting the partner in the box shall be a short. See Rule 4.6 (c).

(b) Screen Balls. Passes so close to the server or the server's partner that the view of the returning side is obstructed. Any serve passing behind the server's partner and the side wall shall be an automatic screen. See Rule 4.10 (a) (4).

(c) Court Hinders. Hits any part of the court that under local rules is a dead ball. See Rule 4.10 (a) (1).

Rule 4.5 Fault Serves. The following serves are faults, and any two in succession result in a hand-out:

(a) Foot Faults. A foot fault results:

(1) When the server leaves the service zone before the served ball passes the short line. See Rule 4.1 (c).

(2) When the server's partner leaves the service box before the served ball passes the short line. See Rule 4.1 (c).

(b) Short Serve. A short serve is any served ball that first hits the front wall and on the rebound hits the floor in front of the back edge of the short line either with or without touching one side wall.

(c) Two-Side Serve. A two-side serve is any ball served that first hits the front wall and on the rebound hits two side walls on the fly.

(d) Ceiling Serve. A ceiling serve is any served ball that touches the ceiling after hitting the front wall either with or without touching one side wall.

(e) Long Serve. A long serve is any served ball that first hits the front wall and rebounds to the back wall before touching the floor.

(f) Out-of-Court Serve. An out-of-court serve is any ball that goes out of the court on the serve. See also Rule 4.9 (f).

Rule 4.6 Out Serves. Any one of the following serves results in a hand-out:

(a) Bounces. Bouncing the ball more than three times while in the service zone before striking the ball. A bounce is counted each time the ball hits the floor within the service zone. Once the server is within the service zone, the ball may be bounced only on the floor within the service zone. Accidental dropping of the ball counts as one bounce.

(b) Missed Ball. Any attempt to strike the ball on the first bounce that results either in a total miss or in touching any part of the server's body other than his serving hand or fist.

(c) Non-front Wall Serve. Any served ball that strikes the server's partner or the ceiling, floor, or side wall before striking the front wall.

(d) Touched Serve. Any served ball that on the rebound from the front wall touches the server, or touches the server's partner while any part of his body is out of the service box, or is intentionally caught. See Rule 4.4 (a).

(e) Out-of-Order Serve. In doubles, when either partner serves out of order or serves using both hands.

(f) Crotch Serve. Any served ball that hits the crotch in the front wall shall be considered the same as a ball that hits the floor and is an out. To be consistent a crotch serve into the back wall is good and in play; as is any served ball that hits front wall, side wall, and crotches another side wall or the back wall.

Rule 4.7 Return of Serve.

(a) Receiving Position. The receiver or receivers must stand at least 5 feet back of the short line, as indicated by the 3-in. vertical line on each side wall, until the ball is struck by server. See Rule 2.1 (b) (5). Any infraction of this rule results in a point for server.

(b) Defective Serve. To eliminate any misunderstanding, the receiving side may not catch or touch a defectively served ball until the serve has been called by the referee or the ball has touched the floor the second time.

(c) Fly Return. In making a fly return, receiver must play ball after it passes over the short line; no part of the foot may extend over short line. A violation results in a point for server.

(d) Legal Return. After the ball is legally served, one of the players on the receiving side must strike the ball either on the fly or after the first bounce and before the ball touches the floor the second time to return the ball to the front wall either directly or after it has touched one or both side walls, the back wall, or the ceiling, or any combination of those surfaces. A returned ball may not touch the floor before touching the front wall.

(e) Failure to Return. The failure to return a serve results in a point for the server.

(f) Touching Receiver. See Rule 4.9 (e).

Rule 4.8 Changes of Serve.

(a) Hand-out. A server is entitled to continue serving until:

(1) Out Serve. The server makes an out serve under Rule 4.6.

(2) Fault Serve. The server makes two fault serves in succession under Rule 4.5.

(3) Hits Partner. The server hits his partner with an attempted return before the ball touches the floor the second time.

(4) Return Failure. The server or his partner fails to keep the ball in play by returning it as required by Rule 4.7 (d).

(5) Avoidable Hinder. The server or his partner commits an avoidable hinder. See Rule 4.11.

(b) Side-out.

(1) In Singles. In singles, retiring the server retires the side.

(2) In Doubles. In doubles, the side is retired when both partners have been put out, except on the first serve as provided in Rule 4.2 (a).

(c) Effect. When the server or the side loses the serve, the server or serving side becomes the receiver, and the receiving side, the server; and so alternately in all subsequent services of the game.

Rule 4.9 Volleys. Each legal return after the serve is called a volley. Play during volleys must accord with the following rules (each violation of (a), (b), or (c) results in a hand-out or point):

(a) One Hand. Only the front or back of one hand may be used at any one time to return the ball. Using two hands to hit a ball is an out. The use of the foot or any portion of the body, other than the hand or fist, is an out.

(b) Wrist Ball. The use of any other part of the body, including the wrist or arm, above the player's hand to return the ball is prohibited.

(c) One Touch. In attempting returns, the ball may be touched only once by one player or returning side. In doubles both partners may swing at, but only one may hit, the ball.

(d) Return Attempts.

(1) In Singles. In singles, if a player swings at but misses the ball in play, the player may repeat his attempts to return the ball until it touches the floor the second time.

(2) In Doubles. In doubles, if one player swings at but misses the ball, both he and his partner may make further attempts to return the ball until it touches the floor the second time. Both partners on a side are entitled to attempts to return the ball.

(3) Hinders. In singles or doubles, if a player swings at but misses the ball in play, and in his, or his partner's, attempt again to play the ball there is an unintentional interference by an opponent, a hinder is called. See Rule 4.10.

(e) Touching Ball. Except as provided in Rule 4.10 (a) (2), any touching of a ball before it touches the floor the second time by a player other than the one making a return is a point or an out against the offending player.

(f) Out-of-Court Ball.

(1) After Return. Any ball returned to the front wall that on the rebound or on the first bounce goes into the gallery or through any opening in a side wall is declared dead and the serve is replayed.

(2) No Return. Any ball not returned to the front wall, but which caroms off a player's hand or fist into the gallery or into any opening in a side wall either with or without touching the ceiling, side or back wall, is an out or point against the player failing to make the return. See also Rule 4.5 (f).

(g) Dry Ball and Gloves. During the game and particularly on service every effort must be made to keep the ball dry. Deliberate wetting results in an out. The ball may be inspected by the referee at any time during a game. If a player's gloves are wet to the extent that they leave wet marks on the ball, the player must change to dry gloves on a referee's time out. If a player wishes to change to dry gloves, he must hold the palms of his hands up to the referee and obtain the referee's permission to change. He may not leave the court without the referee's permission.

(h) Broken Ball. If there is any suspicion that a ball has broken on the serve or during a volley, play continues until the end of the volley. The referee or any player may request the ball be examined. If the referee decides the ball is broken or is otherwise defective, a new ball must be put into play and the point replayed.

(i) Play Stoppage. If a player loses a shoe or other equipment, or foreign objects enter the court, or any other outside interference occurs, the referee must stop the play.

Rule 4.10 Dead-Ball Hinders. Hinders are of two types—"dead-ball" and "avoidable." Dead ball hinders as described in this rule result in the point's being replayed. Avoidable hinders are described in Rule 4.11.

(a) Situations. When called by the referee, the following are dead-ball hinders:

(1) Court Hinders. When the ball hits any part of the court that under local rules is a dead-ball area.

(2) Hitting Opponent. When a returned ball touches an opponent on the fly before it returns to the front wall.

(3) Body Contact. When any body contact with an opponent interferes with seeing or returning the ball.

(4) Screen Ball. When any ball rebounds from the front wall close to the body of a player on the side that has just returned the ball in such a way as to interfere with or prevent the returning side from seeing the ball. See Rule 4.4 (b).

(5) Straddle Ball. When a ball passes between the legs of a player on the side that just returned the ball, if there is no fair chance for the opposing player to see or return the ball.

(6) Other Interference. When any other unintentional interference prevents an opponent from having a fair chance to see or return the ball.

(b) Effect. A call by the referee of a "hinder" stops the play and voids any situation following, such as the ball hitting a player. No player is authorized to call a hinder, except on the back swing, and such a call must be made immediately as provided in Rule 3.5 (b).

(c) Avoidance. While making an attempt to return the ball, a player is entitled to a fair chance to see and to return the ball. It is the duty of the side that has just served or returned the ball to move so that the receiving side may go straight to the ball and not be required to go around an opponent. The referee should be liberal in calling hinders in order to discourage any practice of playing the ball in such a way that an opponent cannot see it until it is too late. It is no excuse that the ball is "killed," unless in the opinion of the referee the player cannot return the ball. Hinders must be called without a claim by a player, especially in close plays and on game points. It is not a hinder when one player hinders his partner.

(d) In Doubles. In doubles, both players on a side are entitled to a fair and unobstructed chance at the ball and either one is entitled to a hinder even though it naturally would be his partner's ball and even though his partner may have attempted to play the ball and have already missed it.

Rule 4.11 Avoidable Hinders. An avoidable hinder results in an out or a point depending upon whether the offender was serving or receiving. Avoidable hinders are called when:

(a) Failure to Move. A player does not move sufficiently to allow his opponent his shot.

(b) Blocking. A player moves into a position that effects a block on the opponent about to return the ball; or, in doubles, one partner moves in front of an opponent as his partner is returning the ball.

(c) Moving into Ball. A player moves in the way and is struck by the ball just played by his opponent.

(d) Pushing. A player deliberately pushes or shoves an opponent during a volley.

Rule 4.12 Rest Periods.

(a) Delays. Deliberate delays exceeding 10 seconds by server or receiver shall result in an out or point against the offender.

(b) During Game. During a game each player in singles, or each side in doubles, either while serving or while receiving may request a "time out" for a towel, to wipe glasses, to change, or to adjust equipment. Each time out must not exceed 30 seconds. No more than three time outs in a game may be granted each singles player or each team in doubles.

(c) Injury. No time out may be charged to a player who is injured during play. An injured player may not be allowed more than a total of 15 minutes of rest. If the injured player is not able to resume play after rests that total 15 minutes, the match must be awarded to the opponent or opponents. On any further injury to the same player, the Commissioner, if present, or the committee, after considering any available medical opinion, must determine whether the injured player may be allowed to continue.

(d) Between Games. A 2-minute rest period is allowed between the first and second games, at which times the players may not leave the court without the approval of the referee. A 10-minute rest period is allowed between the second and third games, at which time the players may leave the court.

(e) Postponed Games. Any games postponed by referee because of weather elements may be resumed with the same score as when postponed.

One-wall and three-wall rules

Basically handball rules for one-wall, three-wall and four-wall are the same, with the following exceptions:

One-wall

1. Court Size. Walls shall be 20 feet in width and 16 feet high, floor 20 feet in width and 34 feet from the wall to the back edge of the long line. There shall be a minimum of 3 feet beyond the long line and 6 feet outside each side line. There shall be a minimum of 6 feet outside each side line and behind the long line to permit movement area for the players.
2. Short Line. Back edge 16 feet from the wall.
3. Service Markers. Lines at least 6 inches long and 1½ inches wide parallel to and midway between the long and short lines, extending in from the side lines.
4. Service Line. The imaginary extension and joining of the service marker lines.
5. Service Zone. Floor area inside and including the short, side, and service lines.
6. Receiving Zone. Floor area in back of short line bounded by and including the long and side lines.

Three-wall

1. Serve. A serve that goes beyond the side walls on the fly is player or side-out. A serve that goes beyond the long line on a fly but within the side walls is that same as a short.

glossary

Ace: Legal serve that eludes the receiver, scoring a point.

Avoidable Hinder: Avoidable interference by one player with another's clear shot. Penalty is loss of serve or point.

Back Court: Court area back of short line.

Back-wall Shot: Shot made from rebound off rear wall.

Block (or Screen): Preventing your opponent from viewing the ball.

Ceiling Shot: Ball hit to ceiling.

Chop: Method of putting "English" on ball.

Court Hinder: Construction obstacle that deflects ball (light fixtures, latches). Point is replayed.

Crotch Ball: Ball striking juncture of two playing surfaces.

Crotch Serve: Serve that strikes juncture of front wall and floor or ceiling. Illegal.

Cutthroat: Game with three players with each server during his turn playing the other two players.

Dead Ball: Any ball out of play, especially following penalty.

Defensive Shot: A return shot usually made to continue volley rather than end it.

Dig: To retrieve a low ball before it goes dead.

Doubles: Game of two teams of two players each.

Drive: Hard hit straight ball to front wall.

"English": To add spin to the ball.

Error: Failure to return an apparently playable ball.

Fault: Illegal serve or other infraction of serving rules.

Feint: Move designed to draw opponent out of position.

Fist Ball: Striking ball with fist (also called punch or bolo ball).

Fly Ball: Shot played on rebound off front wall before it hits floor.

Foot Fault: Illegal placement of foot outside serve zone during serve.

Front Court: Area in front of short line.

Front Line: *See* Service Line

Half-Volley: Ball hit immediately after it bounces off floor (also called trap shot).

Hand-out: Loss of serve by first partner serving for his team in doubles.

Hinder: Unavoidable interference with opponent or flight of ball. No penalty.

Hop: Ball that comes off front wall and, because of spin, curves left or right after bouncing.

Inning: One complete round of play in which both sides serve.

Kill: Shot to front wall that rebounds too close to floor to be returned.

Lob: Softly hit high serve.

Long Serve: Any serve that rebounds to the back wall without first striking the floor.

Offensive Position: Approximately center court.

Offensive Shot: Shot designed to win volley.

Off Hand: Weak hand.

Out: Loss of serve when server misses shot or flubs serve.

Passing Shot: Ball shot out of opponent's reach.

Point: Tally scored by successful server.

Rally: Period of play from time ball is served until one side fails to return ball to front wall.

Receiver: Player to whom ball is served.

Roll-out: Kill shot that does not bounce on rebound but rolls out.

Run-around Shot: Ball angled from one side, to the back, to other side wall.

Screen: *See* Block

Serve: The act of putting ball in play.

Server: Player putting ball in play.

Service Box: The demarcated box 18 inches from side wall in which nonserving member of doubles serving team stands with back to wall during serve.

Service Line: Line parallel to and five feet in front of short line.

Service Zone: Court area between short line and service line (also called service lane).

Shadow Serve: Serve concealed from receiver's view on rebound until it passes server.

Shoot: To attempt kill shots.

Short: Serve that fails to rebound past short line. Illegal.

Short Line: Line halfway between and parallel to front and back walls.

Side-out: Loss of serve by singles player, or, in doubles, by team.

Singles: One player playing against one other.

Straddle Ball: Ball that goes between legs of player.

Three-wall Serve: Serve that hits three walls on the fly. Illegal.

Trap Kill: Trap shot that is killed.

Trap Shot: Ball played just after it rebounds from floor (also called half-volley).

Two-side Serve: Any serve that hits two sides on the fly.

Volley: Any shot played before it strikes floor after it rebounds from front wall.

Wrist Shot: Ball hit with wrist. Illegal.

index